I0419729

Toucans
For Kids

Amazing Animal Books
For Young Readers

By
Rachel Smith

Mendon Cottage Books
JD-Biz Corp Publishing

All Rights Reserved.

No part of this publication may be reproduced in any form or by any means, including scanning, photocopying, or otherwise without prior written permission from JD-Biz Corp

Copyright © 2015. All Images Licensed by Fotolia and 123RF.

Read More Amazing Animal Books

Purchase at Amazon.com

Table of Contents

Introduction

Some birds are beautiful, such as the blue and gold macaw, the dove, and the peacock; other birds are graceful, such as the different types of swan.

The toucan is none of these. It is one of the funniest looking kinds of birds out there, and that includes the kiwi, the ostrich, and the flamingo. A toucan has a huge beak, some of them as long as their body.

This New World bird is one fascinating creature, not only for its beak and bright colors, but also for the way it lives and does things. Not all birds are alike, after all.

What is a toucan?

The toucan is a Central and South American bird that has a huge beak and is typically very colorful. All toucans are from the family Ranphastidae, from the little toucanet to the aracari to the more familiar toco toucan.

A white-throated toucan.

Toucans are birds that have big beaks. This is not the only feature that toucans have, but it is one of the most obvious. They tend to be anywhere from just a bit big to as big as their bodies or bigger, as mentioned before.

Some distant relatives of the toucans are certain woodpeckers and barbets. But the toucans are a distinct family all their own.

Toucans had small, compact bodies. Their wings are short, because toucans don't need to fly very far, and rarely do. This is because they tend to live in forests and jungle, and there are plenty of things to land on in such a place.

They also have four toes with two backwards on each foot. They are strong feet and legs, and this makes them able to spend as long as they do up in trees.

Toucans are not generally sexually dimorphic; this term means that the animals in question are fairly different-looking if they are a boy or girl animal. Toucans look mostly the same, though females' bills might be smaller and blockier. There is only one kind of toucan that is sexually dimorphic, and this is the Seledinera genus.

Beaks are not as heavy as they look. They tend to be fairly light; this is because they are made up of bone struts with spongy keratin (a tough substance that makes up things like fingernails and hair in humans) in between. It's not a solid mass.

Because of the serrated edges of the beak (pointy-looking parts), the people who studied animals in the past thought that they ate fish and were carnivorous. However, it has been proved in the meantime that they actually eat a lot of fruit, and very rarely other things. The toucan is not really a carnivore, as carnivores need meat to survive and toucans simply don't.

The beak of the toucan can help in thermoregulation. Thermoregulation is the way that a creature manages its body heat. This means that the beak helps them make their blood cooler.

It also helps with getting food; because it's so long, it doesn't have to move around as much to get food. This is a way it helps save energy, which can be important to survival for frugivores (fruit-eaters) like the toucan. Food that frugivores eat typically isn't that high in calories, and so they need to take in as much as they can with as small an amount of energy spent as possible. However, the toucan also does sometimes eat small lizards, eggs, and other proteins when given the opportunity.

Some experts also believe the size of the beak scares away smaller birds.

The toucan has a tongue that may be up to six inches long. It is better at tasting things than a human tongue for an interesting reason: it's frayed. This means it has loose parts, and these help the toucan taste things better. This is important because the toucan needs to be able to tell if fruit is good to eat or not.

Toucans also have a unique skeleton. Most animals (at least vertebrates, meaning those who have vertebrae, or a spine, in other words), have a series of joints in their spine. These joints can move, but not nearly as far as an elbow or knee joint, for example. This is because the elbow or knee is a hinge joint, and vertebrae (the little bones that make up the spine) are attached at either end to another vertebra.

In toucans, the tail vertebrae are connected to the rest of the spine with a ball and socket joint. This gives it way more movement than even an elbow or knee; it even tends to have more movement than the ball and socket joints (the thigh bone to the hip bone) in humans.

Toucans can put their tail on top of their head, and this is how they sleep. No other animal has this feature. They generally look like a ball of feathers when sleeping this way.

They live in trees, rarely touching on the ground; they like to stay in holes in trees, and also make their nests in such spots. Toucans lay about 2-21 eggs, and they live in either pairs or flocks of a number of toucans. They are not typically solitary (alone or single) creatures.

What kinds of toucans are there?

There are a number of types of toucans. It starts out with the kind we are most familiar with, the typical toucan, and goes to toucanets, mountain toucans, and aracaris. There are two different kinds of toucanet genera (a more specific group than family or kingdom, but not as specific as species).

A saffron toucanet.

First, there are the typical toucans. There are about eight kinds, and they tend to be the ones that people see the most and know the most about. This is where you'll see those enormous colorful bills, and they are often black with bright colors. They also are bigger than some of the other genera. The most well-known kinds are the toco and the choco toucans, though the toco toucan is the best-known. It's usually what you'll see a picture of if someone wants a picture of a toucan.

Then there are the green toucanets. They are smaller than typical toucans, and they are pretty much all green, though in differing amounts. For a long time, they've been known to have six species, but more recently it's been suggested that the emerald toucanet is actually seven different species of toucanet.

Dichromatic toucanets are next. Like the green toucanets, they are smaller than the typical toucan. All the males have green upper parts, a red undertail, and a green or greenish-blue patch of unfeather skin around their eyes. The reason they're called dichromatic is that the females always look different than the males in color, unlike the other kinds of toucans. 'Di' refers to there being two, and 'chromatic' refers to color.

The mountain toucans live, unsurprisingly, in the mountains. Specifically, they live in rainforests in the Andes mountain range in South America. They are all colored in a similar way to each other, with blue-gray, olive-brown, red, yellow, and black parts. There are only four species of mountain toucans.

The last kind: the aracaris. These toucans are made up of fourteen different species, all with bright and contrasting colors. They are all medium size. The saffron toucanet is a member despite not being called an aracari because when it was named, it was originally believed to have its own genus. Instead, however, it was discovered more recently to belong to the aracaris. The smallest kind of toucan is the lettered aracari, a very small bird indeed, weighing about one hundred and thirty grams and being only twenty-nine centimeters long. The interesting thing about aracaris, as compared to their fellow toucans, is that they often live in much larger groups than other toucans.

The history of toucans and humans

Altogether, humans have not affected toucans much. Unlike animals that were domesticated or commonly hunted, the toucan mostly lives outside of the human area. While they have had some issues with habitat destruction, humans mostly leave toucans alone.

A gray-breasted mountain toucan.

Humans have been known to do good things for toucans too. For example, there are shelters that take care of toucans that are injured or nearly kidnapped by poachers.

Poachers are a bit of a problem with toucans, though not as big as it is for, say, rhinos or the like. Because are so colorful and considered exotic, they migh be taken to be a rich person's exotic pet. But the problem with taking a wild animal and making it a pet is not only that it will be miserable, but that it will never really be domesticated like a cat or a dog. It takes generations of breeding to reach that sort of attitude towards humans.

This is why we don't go outside and steal wild rabbits or squirrels. A wild dog that is simply a dog abandoned by owners may be able to be rehabilitated, or made to be able to be in a house or with people again. A wolf that is taken from the wild will never be truly safe to have around humans.

While a toucan is not the most dangerous animal in the world, it can hurt people, and it's not so tiny either. It would be very unhappy trapped in a cage in someone's home.

However, toucans also live in zoos, typically in aviaries, which are a special exhibit for birds. Often, they will share a very large space with many other tropical birds from their area. Toucans in most zoos are quite happy because zookeepers and the people who are in charge of the zoo know what to do to keep them happy; illegal owners do not typically know how to keep an exotic pet happy.

In popular culture, the toucan is used in different ways.

For one, there is the Brazilian Social Democracy Party; their logo has a toucan on it, and because of this, they are often called tucanos, which is the Portuegese of calling them toucans. It's a blue and toucan that looks fairly normal.

A less normal toucan is Toucan Sam, who belongs the Kellogg company. He is put on boxes of cereal, and he is a pretty bird, with raibow rings along his beak and blue feathers, but he doesn't seem to particularly match any kind of toucan. Also, he uses his wings like hands, which is fine for cartoon characters, but which would never work in real life. Still, he's a fitting mascot for a fruit-flavored cereal, since toucans eat fruit almost exclusively.

There is also a Tucana constellation in the sky. You can't see it from the Northern hemisphere nor the Eastern hemisphere. A constellation is a grouping of stars that people say looks like something; for instance, the Ancient Greeks often named their star groups after heroes in their myths, such as Gemini and Andromeda. The Tucana constellation is named after the toucan.

Toucans are also in some cartoons and even movies. Like most animal characters, and especially since toucans are not particularly easy to train, they are animated most of the time.

Advertisements (pictures and other things used to tell you about a product or service) have had toucans in them too. For instance, the beer company Guiness used to have a toucan in some of their beer advertisements in the 1930s and 1940s.

Altogether, the toucan has not had the horrible experience with humans that a lot of other animals have, such as the passenger pigeon or the elephant.

Toco toucan

The toco toucan, also known as the common toucan or simply toucan, is probably the best known species of toucan in the world. It's the largest, and fairly distinctive. It's the most likely type of toucan you'd see in a zoo.

A toco toucan.

A toco toucan has an orange beak which is very long. It has blue around its eyes, white below its beak and places on its tail and wings, and otherwise is pretty much all black. It's a beautiful bird, even with its funny-looking beak.

Toco toucans live throughout places in Bolivia, Peru, Paraguay, Brazil, and Argentina, among other places. Unlike some of their brethren, they live in semi-open spaces, and this is probably why they are the most known: they are easiest to spot, due to size, location, and bright colors. It also lives in several places that are more isolated from the main habitat area.

The toco toucan makes noises; these include the bill-clack, which it makes with its beak, the rattling call it makes, and the deep croaking. The deep croaking is done fairly frequently, and does not sound anything like songbirds or many other animals that live in somewhat colder climates. However, it does not quite reach the shocking chainsaw sound of a puffin.

A bird like the toco toucan cannot fly very far. When it does fly, it tests to either have a lot of quick wing flaps or glide, and it can do neither of these for very long. This is because its wings are short and rounded; it evolved to fly in a place with tons of perches, so it never needed to fly very far at all. They more typically hop from spot to spot.

The long beak it has is not only good for reaching fruit, which is its main food, but also in scaring predators. The toco toucan deals with animals such as the weasel, the jaguar, and various snakes. But the toco toucan can be a predator too: it often goes after small birds, their eggs, lizards, frogs, and insects.

Toco toucans live either in pairs, or in small groups. It is a social animal, but not nearly as social as rabbits or mice, for example. They tend to nest seasonally, meaning there is a specific point in the year when the female wants to fertilize her eggs. The male and female work together to keep the eggs incubated, meaning that they keep them warm so that the babies inside survive. Typically, the female lays 2-4, and the nest is in a hollow in a tree.

Their beaks are the hugest compared to body size out of all birds except the sword-billed hummingbird, though not all count the hummingbird. A lot of people have speculated on why this is: some think it attracts mates, others think it helps peel fruit, and still others think it helps them scare other creatures.

The toco toucan is not endangered. In fact, it has been put in the Least Concern category. They are very abundant, and along with their fellow typical toucan, the keel-billed toucan, are often kept in captivity.

They typically do well in zoos and other places, as long as they have enough fruit and don't eat rats or mice.

Yellow-browed toucanet

Out of all toucans, the yellow-browed toucanet is the one that we know the least about. It lives in Peru in the humid rainforest on the east Andean slope. Unlike the toco toucan, which has a vast range, the yellow-browed toucanet lives in one small area; this is called being endemic to the area.

But the yellow-browed toucanet is not just endemic; it is nearly impossible to reach. It lives in three small areas within the east Andean slope in Peru, all almost inaccessible (impossible to get to) to humans. What little we have seen of them tells us they are pretty birds, all green except for the yellow 'brows' and a blue band that goes around its chest.

The worry is that the yellow-browed toucanet is endangered due to habitat loss; since there is only a tiny amount of space they will live in, the destruction of that habitat is disastrous for them. They could easily become extinct if all three areas were completely cleared out by loggers and the like.

Its call is a short, dry-sounding noise, sort of a rattling sound.

Emerald toucanet

The emerald toucanet is one funny looking bird. Related to the yellow-browed toucanet and just about as green, the emerald toucanet lives near the Andes mountains, but not in Peru.

An emerald toucanet, sometimes mistakenly called an emerald toucan.

Emerald toucanets prefer a home in humid forests or woodland. This type of toucan also puts its eggs in a tree hollow, but both parents feed the babies. Baby emerald toucanet are blind and naked at bird, possessing short beaks and special pads on their feet to protect them from the nest, which can be kind of rough, especially to sensitive babies.

When the babies leave the nest after about six weeks, the parents will often continue to feed them for the first few weeks.

Emerald toucanets like to travel in small groups, usually about 5-10 birds who follow each other in fast bursts of flight. They fly more than the toco toucan, and are better at it.

The emerald toucanet is thought to possibly be seven different species, differing depending on where they live throughout South America and Central America. Slight differences in appearance are there, but not all believe this is a reason to call them by separate names.

They are only about thirty to thirty-five centimeters long. Toucanets tend to be smaller than other kinds of toucans, and the emerald toucanet is no exception.

Plate-billed mountain toucan

The plate-billed mountain toucan lives in Ecuador and Colombia, in the Andes mountains. It mostly lives in scrubland and the humid forest. The interesting thing about this bird, and its fellow mountain toucans, is that it lives at a higher altitude (level above sea) than its other relatives.

Plate-billed mountain toucans are about 45 to 53 centimeters long, making them not small, but not the biggest either. They are pretty colorful, though not as bright as some of their fellow toucans. The plate-billed mountain toucan has blue, red, olive green, reddish brown, yellow, black, and various other colors all over its body; their beak is black, though it also has red and ivory colors on it.

It is easily the loudest of the mountain toucans. The male and the female make different noises back and forth, the female's sound a little bit drier sounding. There's a big difference between their sounds, the male's more like tryyyyyk and the female's more like t't't't't't.

It's very good for its environment, since the plate-billed mountain toucan spreads seeds from the fruits it eats in its poo.

The danger for the plate-billed mountain toucan, as well as for the other mountain toucans, is deforestation. Their habitat is being destroyed.

However, it is only considered near threatened, and not in danger of going extinct any time soon.

Collared aracari

The collared aracari is a toucan 39 to 42 centimeters in length. This makes it a decent size toucan; its fellow aracari, the lettered aracari, is the smallest toucan, and the collared aracari is much bigger.

A collared aracari.

It has very interesting colors, like most toucans. For one thing, it has black skin around its eyes, which becomes red above it. It also is yellow on its underparts, and in the middle of its chest, it has a round black spot. Its beak is also fairly colorful. It's named for the band of reddish color around its neck, which looks kind of like a collar.

The collared aracari tends to live in groups of six to fifteen birds, showing that it is definitely a social animal, and would be very unhappy living alone. These birds fly fast, and move in a group.

This kind of toucan lays about three eggs, and it tends to like old woodpecker nests to lay them in. Both parents help keep the eggs warm.

They are fairly unusual, because they live in a social group throughout the year; most toucans don't do that. Specifically, they don't roost together, which is what the collared aracaris do. Around six aracaris may be together in one hole in a tree.

Conclusion

The toucan, that crazy-looking bird that has fascinated animal experts for centuries, will probably always have a place in the world. It's a beautiful, interesting creature, and as long as we don't destroy its habitat, it should remain a common creature for many centuries to come.

Author Bio

Rachel Smith is a young author who enjoys animals. Once, she had a rabbit which was very nervous, and chewed through her leash and tried to escape. She's also had several pet mice, which were the funniest little animals to watch. She lives in Ohio with her family and writes in her spare time.

Publisher

JD-Biz Corp

P O Box 374

Mendon, Utah 84325

http://www.jd-biz.com/

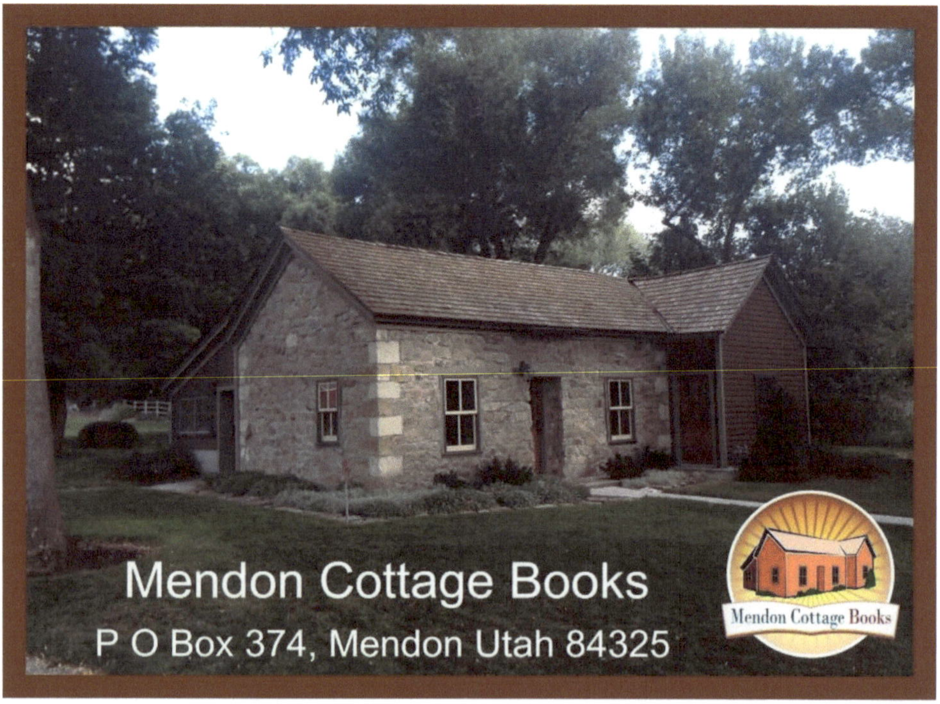

Mendon Cottage Books

P O Box 374, Mendon Utah 84325

Top Ten Dog Breeds For Kids
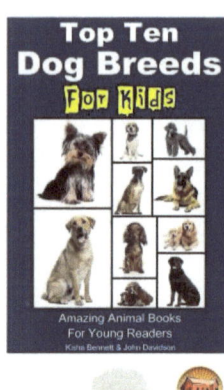
Amazing Animal Books For Young Readers
Kisha Bennett & John Davidson

German Shepherds

Dog Books for Kids
K. Bennett

Bulldogs

Dog Books for Kids
K. Bennett

Dachshund

Dog Books for Kids
K. Bennett

Poodles
Dog Books for Kids
K. Bennett

Labrador Retrievers

Dog Books for Kids
K. Bennett

Rottweilers

Dog Books for Kids
K. Bennett

Boxers

Dog Books for Kids
K. Bennett

Golden Retrievers

Dog Books for Kids
K. Bennett

Puppies
Dog Books For Kids

Amazing Animal Books
By John Davidson

Beagles

Dog Books for Kids
K. Bennett

Yorkshire Terriers

Dog Books for Kids
K. Bennett

Dogs
Top Ten Dog Breeds For Kids

Amazing Animal Books For Young Readers
Zahra Jazeel & John Davidson

Cats For Kids

Amazing Animal Books For Young Readers
K. Bennett & John Davidson

Foxes For Kids
Amazing Animal Books For Young Readers
Zahra Jazeel & John Davidson

Wolves For Kids

Amazing Animal Books For Young Readers
By John Davidson and Virginia Fidler

www.ingramcontent.com/pod-product-compliance
Lightning Source LLC
Chambersburg PA
CBHW050918290526
45792CB00002B/806